My Journal of Prayers and Answers

God Responds to My Requests

We hope you enjoy this book! We love creating a variety of Christian themed books including journals, planners, and blank books for both adults and children.

For all our products visit us on Amazon at:

GingerLark Studio

But as for me, I will look to the Lord;
I will wait for the God of my salvation.
My God will hear me.

Micah 7:7

Throughout the Bible, God promises to answer the prayers of those who are faithful to him. Prayer is powerful and changes things that wouldn't change otherwise. But how often when you pray, even when you take the time to write down your prayers, do you fail to notice God's responses? Maybe the answer takes so long that you've forgotten your request. Or, perhaps the answer comes in a way you weren't expecting so you fail to recognize it. What about when you pray for something and the situation doesn't improve but gets worse? How do you interpret that answer?

By taking the time to record our prayers, review them, and note how God responds, in whatever form that takes, we build a testimony of our trust in God and His faithfulness to us. And we also get to notice that sometimes His faithfulness doesn't include fixing all our problems, but means sending His Spirit to bring peace and encouragement during challenging times.

The discipline and grace of recording your prayers and God's responses will never guarantee the exact answers you want or hope for. God may have a different plan than your desires. But documenting God's answers gives you the opportunity to cultivate a habit of watchfulness and appreciation as God works in your life. Keeping a journal of answered prayer leaves you with a treasure of memories of God's love and kindness, compassion and provision.

Sample Use

Date	Prayer Requests	Date	God's Answers
10/4/19	Lord, it's so difficult at work right now. Please bless my search for a new job and help me keep a good attitude while I wait.	1/18/20	Today my boss gave her 2 week notice & I was offered her position! Thank you God for giving me patience and a great new opportunity!

♥ Scripture that speaks to my Heart ♥
Psalm 27:14 Wait patiently for the LORD; be strong and courageous.
Wait patiently for the LORD.

But God has surely heard; He has attended to the sound of my prayer.

Psalm 66:19

Date	Prayer Requests	Date	God's Answers

Date	Prayer Requests	Date	God's Answers

Date	Prayer Requests	Date	God's Answers

Lord,

Thank You that You never forget me and that You hear each one of my prayers.

Please help me to hear Your gentle whispers, to recognize Your answers to my prayers, and to feel Your presence throughout my life.

And even when You don't answer in the ways that I want, Lord, I will still have faith in You and love You because I know that You loved me first.

In Jesus' Name, Amen

Date	Prayer Requests	Date	God's Answers

Date	Prayer Requests	Date	God's Answers

♥ Scripture that speaks to my Heart ♥

Date	Prayer Requests	Date	God's Answers

♥ **Scripture that speaks to my Heart** ♥

> "True prayer is neither a mere mental exercise nor a vocal performance. It is far deeper than that - it is spiritual transaction with the Creator of Heaven and Earth."
>
> ~Charles Spurgeon~

Date	Prayer Requests	Date	God's Answers

♥ Scripture that speaks to my Heart ♥

Is any one of you suffering? He should pray. Is anyone cheerful? He should sing praises.

James 5:13

Date	Prayer Requests	Date	God's Answers

♥ Scripture that speaks to my Heart ♥

Date	Prayer Requests	Date	God's Answers

♥ Scripture that speaks to my Heart ♥

Date	Prayer Requests	Date	God's Answers

♥ Scripture that speaks to my Heart ♥

Heavenly Father,

Help me to see all the blessings You pour
out on me every moment of every day.

Forgive me for my frequent failure to
trust You or to thank You
for Your faithfulness.

I am grateful that You continually
watch over me me even when I fail to
recognize that You are with me. Thank
You for Your everlasting loving
kindness.

In Jesus' Name, Amen

Date	Prayer Requests	Date	God's Answers

♥ Scripture that speaks to my Heart ♥

Date	Prayer Requests	Date	God's Answers

Date	Prayer Requests	Date	God's Answers

♥ **Scripture that speaks to my Heart** ♥

"God shapes the world by prayer. Prayers are deathless. The lips that uttered them may be closed in death, the heart that felt them may have ceased to beat, but the prayers live before God, and God's heart is set on them and prayers outlive the lives of those who uttered them; outlive a generation, outlive an age, outlive a world."

~E. M. Bounds~

Date	Prayer Requests	Date	God's Answers

♥ Scripture that speaks to my Heart ♥

Call to Me and I will answer and show you great and unsearchable things you do not know.

Jeremiah 33:3

Date	Prayer Requests		Date	God's Answers
___	_____		___	_____
	_____			_____
	_____			_____
	_____			_____
___	_____		___	_____
	_____			_____
	_____			_____
	_____			_____
___	_____		___	_____
	_____			_____
	_____			_____
	_____			_____
___	_____		___	_____
	_____			_____
	_____			_____
	_____			_____
___	_____		___	_____
	_____			_____
	_____			_____
	_____			_____

♥ Scripture that speaks to my Heart ♥

_____
_____
_____
_____
_____

Date	Prayer Requests	Date	God's Answers

♥ Scripture that speaks to my Heart ♥

Date	Prayer Requests	Date	God's Answers

♥ Scripture that speaks to my Heart ♥

Father God,

I have no idea what I'll face in the coming hours, days or weeks.

But You already know.

Lift me up, Lord, when I encounter obstacles, disappointments, and heart break.

Remind me that You are at work in every circumstance. I can cast my burdens on You and You will sustain me. You are my source of peace and strength.

In Jesus' Name, Amen

Date	Prayer Requests	Date	God's Answers

♥ Scripture that speaks to my Heart ♥

Date	Prayer Requests	Date	God's Answers

♥ Scripture that speaks to my Heart ♥

Date	Prayer Requests	Date	God's Answers

♥ Scripture that speaks to my Heart ♥

He answers prayer; so sweetly that I stand
amid the blessings of His wondrous hand
and marvel at the miracle I see,
The favors that His love hath wrought in me.
pray on for the impossible, and dare
upon thy banner this brave motto bear,
"My Father answers prayer."

~Rosalind Goforth~

Date	Prayer Requests		Date	God's Answers

♥ **Scripture that speaks to my Heart** ♥

Be anxious for nothing, but in everything, by prayer and petition, with thanksgiving, present your requests to God. And the peace of God, which surpasses all understanding, will guard your hearts and your minds in Christ Jesus.

Philippians 4:6-7

Date	Prayer Requests	Date	God's Answers

Date	Prayer Requests	Date	God's Answers

Date	Prayer Requests	Date	God's Answers

Lord,

You are All-Knowing and All-Powerful. You are merciful and wise and full of grace. You are the God of all comfort.

You hear the sighs and cries of my heart, so You comfort me.

You know all of my needs, so You provide for me.

Thank You for listening every time I come to You in prayer.

In Jesus' Name, Amen

Date	Prayer Requests	Date	God's Answers

Date	Prayer Requests	Date	God's Answers

♥ Scripture that speaks to my Heart ♥

Date	Prayer Requests	Date	God's Answers

♥ Scripture that speaks to my Heart ♥

"I never prayed sincerely and earnestly for anything but it came at some time — no matter at how distant a day, somehow, in some shape, probably the last I would have devised, it came."

-Adoniram Judson-

Date	Prayer Requests	Date	God's Answers

♥ **Scripture that speaks to my Heart** ♥

Answer me when I call, O
God of my righteousness!

You have relieved my distress;
show me grace and
hear my prayer.

Psalm 4:1

Date	Prayer Requests	Date	God's Answers

♥ Scripture that speaks to my Heart ♥

Date	Prayer Requests		Date	God's Answers

Date	Prayer Requests	Date	God's Answers

Father God,

You call for me to be joyful in hope, patient in affliction, and persistent in prayer. On my own, I so often fail at this.

Father, please help me daily to grow in joy, hope and patience. Help me to cultivate a persistent prayer life so I can draw nearer to You.

In Jesus' Name, Amen

Date	Prayer Requests		Date	God's Answers

Date	Prayer Requests	Date	God's Answers

Date	Prayer Requests	Date	God's Answers

♥ Scripture that speaks to my Heart ♥

> "What a mighty force prayerful praying is.
> Real prayer helps God and man.
> God's Kingdom is advanced by it.
> The greatest good comes to man by it.
> Prayer can do anything that God can do."
>
> ~E. M. Bounds~

Date	Prayer Requests	Date	God's Answers

♥ Scripture that speaks to my Heart ♥

Rejoice at all times.
Pray without ceasing.
Give thanks in every
circumstance, for this is
God's will for you in
Christ Jesus.

1 Thessalonians 5:16–18

Date	Prayer Requests	Date	God's Answers

Date	Prayer Requests	Date	God's Answers

Date	Prayer Requests	Date	God's Answers

Heavenly Father,

You are the God of hope who comforts me in the middle of difficult circumstances. Without You, Lord, I'm not sure I can face the hardships I see around me.

Your word is a lamp to my feet and a light to my path. When I am weak, You renew my strength. When I am overwhelmed by sadness or worry, You give me joy and peace as I believe in You.

You give me overflowing hope!

Thank You, Lord!

In Jesus' Name, Amen

Date	Prayer Requests	Date	God's Answers

Date	Prayer Requests	Date	God's Answers

♥ Scripture that speaks to my Heart ♥

Date	Prayer Requests	Date	God's Answers

♥ Scripture that speaks to my Heart ♥

"Fear not because your prayer is stammering,
your words feeble, and your language poor.
Jesus can understand you."

-J. C. Ryle-

Date	Prayer Requests	Date	God's Answers

♥ Scripture that speaks to my Heart ♥

But to those of you who will listen, I say: Love your enemies, do good to those who hate you, bless those who curse you, pray for those who mistreat you.

Luke 6: 27-28

Date	Prayer Requests	Date	God's Answers

Date	Prayer Requests	Date	God's Answers

♥ Scripture that speaks to my Heart ♥

Date	Prayer Requests	Date	God's Answers

♥ Scripture that speaks to my Heart ♥

Lord,

You are the source of every wonderful thing in this world. You make the sun rise on the evil and the good, and send rain on the just and the unjust.

Lord, I ask You to bless the people I care about – my family, my friends, my co-workers.
And as difficult as this is, I ask You to bless my enemies and those who cause conflict in my life.

Lord, I pray that You draw all of these people into Your kingdom, that they will know Your love, and that Christ will rule in their hearts.

In Jesus' Name, Amen

Date	Prayer Requests	Date	God's Answers

Date	Prayer Requests	Date	God's Answers

♥ Scripture that speaks to my Heart ♥

Date	Prayer Requests	Date	God's Answers

"We may expect answers to prayer, and should not be easy without them any more than we should be if we had written a letter to a friend upon important business, and had received no reply."

-Charles Spurgeon-

Date	Prayer Requests	Date	God's Answers

♥ Scripture that speaks to my Heart ♥

Therefore confess your sins to each other and pray for each other so that you may be healed. The prayer of a righteous man has great power to prevail.

James 5:16

Date	Prayer Requests	Date	God's Answers

♥ Scripture that speaks to my Heart ♥

Date	Prayer Requests	Date	God's Answers

♥ Scripture that speaks to my Heart ♥

May the Lord bless you and
keep you;

May the Lord cause His face
to shine upon you and be
gracious to you;

May the Lord lift up His
countenance toward you and
give you peace.

Numbers 6:24-26

Made in the USA
Lexington, KY
11 August 2019